RUMPELSTILTSKIN'S RULES
FOR MAKING YOUR FARTHINGS GROW

BY SUSAN LAUBACH

Susan Laubach
165 West End Ave, 4R
New York NY 10023
Susanlaubach1@gmail.com

Published by eBookIt.com
http://www.eBookIt.com

ISBN: 978-1-4566-3392-9 (ebook)
ISBN: 978-1-4566-3397-4 (paperback)

TABLE OF CONTENTS

INTRODUCTION

I developed this project for a few reasons. One, having taught Creative Dramatics to elementary and middle-school children, I am aware of how firmly the themes of stories remain in the creators' heads long after the participants move on to higher grades and more complicated lives.

Therefore, utilizing drama in the form of familiar but somewhat skewed fairy tales seemed a good way to cement some informal but, in my opinion, important "rules" for future investors.

Second, I recently heard (and fervently hope) that Financial Literacy is now part of the Education Department's Core Curriculum. It is my belief that understanding basic issues regarding the stock market fits into that structure.

Third, for many years I taught several levels of investment education to students aged 18 to 74, and during that time it became clear to me that beginning investors would rather hear an illustrative story than read a balance sheet or an income statement or a financial analyst's report. No surprise there.

I would suggest using this package in the following way:

1. The group leader should read the fairy tales to get a feel for the use of the stories which illustrate the concepts.

2. After each story, please consult the study guide if things are unclear in the stories and please, PLEASE contact me (contact information below) with anything that is not understood clearly. I will add explanatory information as needed.

3. It may be useful to read the stories aloud to your ultimate audience before embarking on the dramatic presentation.

4. Ask for volunteers to act out the fairy tale characters, duplicate and pass out the scripts and schedule a staged reading.

5. It might work well to do one story and concept at a time (e.g. at weekly sessions). This would give the leader the opportunity to discuss each "rule" and determine if it was well-understood by the participants.

6. The group could stage a full production of all the fairy tales at the end of a semester or similar time period.

NOTE: I welcome all suggestions for the Study Guide and can be reached at susanlaubach1@gmail.com.

Rumpelstiltskin's Rules for Making Your Farthings Grow

1. Slow but steady wins the race.
2. Always ask, what can go wrong with an investment?
3. Know the difference between a loaner to and an owner of a company.
4. Always understand how a company makes its money.
5. Never pay too much for shares of a company's stock.
6. Don't expect your investments to spin straw into gold. That is: Don't expect more from your investment portfolio than is reasonable.

CHAPTER ONE

HOW A PUBLIC COMPANY IS BORN
From a cottage in the woods to the next Marriott Corporation

No doubt you've all heard the story of Goldilox (also called "Goldy"), the bratty little blonde who, while skipping through the woods one day, knocked on the door of the home of the three bears. You may not know what really happened *after* the whole porridge-eating, chair-sitting, bed-sleeping debacle.

Even though no one answered when she knocked, Goldilox pushed open the door and began to wander through the empty house. You know the part about her eating from the three bowls of porridge and choosing to scarf down the smallest one, then sitting in the three chairs, declaring that the smallest chair, like the smallest bowl of porridge, was…"Just right!"

And you know that Goldilox didn't stop there. In one of the bedrooms, she found a bed comfortable enough to fall asleep on which she *actually did,* saying it was…"Just right…" too.

So rude! This girl really had nerve.

When the bears came home, of course they found her, and of course they chased her from their house, slamming the front door after her.

Once Goldy got over the shock of being awakened by three bears and chased into the woods, she looked back at their little house and said to herself,

"Self, whatever possessed you to simply walk into that little house, even though you knew there was no one at home? I'm not usually so rude."

Goldy paused and thought for a minute. Then she said, again to herself, "Self, there's something about this place, something so inviting about it, that I just couldn't resist."

She stood and looked at the home of the three bears.

"It is so cute...and so cozy. This house of the three bears has everything a guest could want - good food, comfy place to sit, soft bed..."

Goldy pondered this, then again said to herself, this time with great excitement, "Oh my goodness, Self! I just got this really, really big idea!"

She ran back to the little house of the three bears and knocked hard, *bang bang bang*, on its front door. This time, she waited for someone to answer before walking in. It was the youngest of the three, Baby Bear. He was not happy to see that Goldilox had returned.

"So, what is it this time, Blondie?" he said. "I'm really annoyed with you because Mama Bear says I have to change the sheets on my little bed and that I can't have any porridge because that girl - that's *you*, Missy- ate all we had."

"We need to talk," Goldy said, and she pushed right past Baby Bear, calling out, "Yoo hoo! Bear people! I'm back!"

Baby Bear's parents, Mama and Papa Bear, came into the room, startled at this second home invasion by Goldilox.

"You again? Why are you here?" they asked angrily.

"Because I have a Big Idea for you," Goldy said.

"Haven't you caused enough trouble for one day?" said Papa Bear.

"Hear me out," said Goldy. She gestured for the bears to sit while she paced back and forth in front of them.

"I know I shouldn't have come inside when you weren't home," she said, "but there's something special about your house. It's all so..so...just right."

Smoothing her skirt, Goldy looked around the little living room. Then she said, "I'm pretty sure it would be just right for *my* mama and papa and all their friends, too."

"*Whaaaaaat?*" chorused all three bears, rising as a group from the sofa.

"What are you talking about?" Papa Bear bellowed. "Are we going to come home and find your whole family here?"

"If you like my idea, it's entirely possible," said Goldy.

"Joan..." began Papa in an exasperated voice. (That was Mama Bear's name, Joan) "We're moving! We're putting this house on the market and we're moving into town! This is the final straw."

Mama Bear nodded vigorously in agreement.

"You're right, George," she said. That was Papa Bear's name, George. "I can't take any more of these break-ins."

"This has happened before?" asked Goldy

"Are you kidding?" cried Papa Bear. "It happens all the time! First it was that girl in the red outfit. Said she wanted to rest awhile before going to her grandma's house."

"Then those two little kids came tearing through here," interjected Baby Bear. "...claiming they got lost looking for a path made of *breadcrumbs.*"

"Don't forget that fellow saying he worked for the Prince," said Mama Bear.

"Ha!" said Papa Bear. "He wanted Joan to try on *shoes*, for heaven's sake." He sighed. "And now *you.*"

Papa Bear sat heavily back onto the sofa and held his head in his paws. "It's just been too much," he added.

"Too much," agreed Mama Bear, joining him.

Goldy sat daintily on Baby Bear's chair and said with great authority, "Location, location, location, Bears. You've got a *great* location. And this place is charming. If you're serious about moving, I think I can help."

She pulled her chair closer to the sofa.

"Please just listen to my Big Idea," she said. "Actually, I should introduce myself first. I'm called Goldilox, but that's not my real name. My real name is Ethel."

Running her fingers through her hair, she continued, "I'm called Goldilox not because of these long blonde curls but because I have a knack for making *money*. Lots of it. My special talent (everyone has at least one, you know) is spotting extraordinary business opportunities and bringing them to the public. I've done it a hundred times..."

Then Goldilox told the Bears that her idea was to turn their cottage into a country inn, a hotel where people would get a bed in which to sleep and breakfast in the morning. They'd call it a "B n B" for Bed and Breakfast.

"The first, I hope, of a nationwide chain." Goldilox said. In the air, she wrote, THE THREE BEARS B'N'B. Then she said, "Trust me, Bears. This will *work*."

The bears were silent. Finally, Baby Bear spoke.

"I don't get it. Do you, Papa? Mama?" He looked at Goldy accusingly. "And you are sitting in *my* chair."

Goldy stood and began to pace in front of the bears. Papa Bear was puzzled. He asked,

"And just *how* would this thing work? We don't know anything about inns or business, and we have no money."

Goldy responded, "I'll put up the money. And the business expertise. You'll use the money to expand the kitchen, add some rooms, maybe a pool and tennis courts!"

Papa Bear turned to his wife and said, "You know, Joan, this is rather a capital idea."

Goldy cried, "You're right, Papa Bear! I'm putting up the **capital**, which is another word for money in the business world. How did you know that?"

Papa Bear, who hadn't known that at all, looked pleased.

He said to his little family, "This could be quite an adventure!"

Again, Goldy was thrilled with his response. "Right again, Papa Bear! I'm an adventure capitalist, **venture capitalist** for short. I'm so impressed that you know so much about business already!"

Mama Bear said proudly, "George is very good at these things."

"Then you both agree?" Goldy asked.

"I think," Papa Bear said, looking at his wife, "we agree. Right, Joan?"

"You are always right, Papa Bear. Yes, we agree," she said to Goldy.

17

"No one asked *me*," muttered Baby Bear.

Goldy said, "Wonderful! Now we're partners and we're all going to make a fortune. We'll share in our new company's ownership, fifty fifty. Half for you Bears and half for me, Goldilox."

She turned to Baby Bear. "Does that suit you, Baby Bear?"

"Uh, sure," Baby Bear said grudgingly. "That sounds good to me, too, I guess. Fifty fifty, like you said."

Mama Bear asked, "But how will you divide it up? The Inn, I mean? We'll each get a bedroom, you'll get the kitchen...like that?"

Papa Bear said, "That won't work. Don't forget we're going to be a chain of Three Bears B&Bs, not just this one."

"So if we build, say, three more inns, we'll each get an inn?" asked Mama Bear.

"No, dear," he said. "That won't work either. What if we have five more inns or even ten more? We'll have to divide up the whole company, no matter how big it gets, right, Goldy?"

"Indeed," said Goldy.

"So my and Joan's share, plus yours will add up to...ownership in the whole company, no matter how big it gets, right?" Papa Bear asked.

"Right again!" Goldy said.

"Just to be clear," said Papa Bear. "You own half and we own half of...what? What is this new company worth? In money, I mean?"

Goldy said, "We can make up any value for it now. Let's say our company is worth $100 and that $100 is made up of 100 parts. We'll be equal partners so I'll have 50 parts and you, Joan, and George will have the other 50 parts."

Papa Bear mulled this over for a minute. Then he said, "Okay! I say, okay. What do you say, Joan?"

"Just so I understand, Goldy," Mama Bear said, "you're saying our new company is worth $100 and by dividing it into parts, you end up with 50 parts and we end up with 50 parts?"

"Yes," said Goldy. "But let's call them 'shares' not 'parts', because we're sharing in the company's ownership. You, George and Joan, own half the shares; I own the other half."

"That makes sense to me," Papa Bear said. He turned to his wife. "You, Joan?'

"Yes, it does, George," she said.

"You, Baby?" Papa Bear asked.

"Don't I get any shares, Pop?" Baby Bear asked.

"Wait until you're a little older, Baby...maybe we'll be able to get you your own shares someday," he answered.

Goldy looked at her new partners with delight and said, "Trust me, Bears, these shares are going to be worth a lot of money! We're going to get rich!"

And indeed, they did. Time passed and, just as Goldilox had predicted, the Three Bears B'N'B Country Inn thrived. In fact, after just a few years, it was such a smashing success that the three partners decided to use the money they'd made to build several more inns. They called their group of inns "The 3 B's Just Right B&B's." The Bears and Goldy now had a thriving chain of businesses.

One day, Goldy called a meeting with her partners in the executive dining room. Over veggie burgers and sweet potato fries, she said to the Bears, "I've called you all here today so I could tell you personally that I have decided it is time for me to take at least part of my money out of our business and to move on."

"Oh, no!" cried the Bears.

"Let me explain. Baby Bear is grown now..." Goldy began.

"Please," Baby Bear said, "call me Bob."

"Of course. Bob. You three can run the Inn business by yourselves now."

"But we need you, Goldy," said Mama Bear. "We need your expertise."

"We need your money," added Papa Bear. "We want to modernize the kitchens, put phones in the bathrooms of the Inns...and frankly, we don't have enough cash to buy your half of the company from you right now."

Goldy said, "I've got an idea about that. We'll raise cash by selling half of the business to other people, the PUBLIC."

"We can do that?" asked Bob Bear.

"Yup," Goldy said. "What we need to do is to get in touch with Rumpelstiltskin - an old friend - and he'll..."

"Wait a minute," Papa Bear said. "Isn't he the little guy who spins straw into gold?"

"He's the one. My pal Rumpelstiltskin (I call him Rump) is managing director of the investment banking firm, Rumpelstiltskin NeverRipOff. It's his business to buy and sell shares of companies to people."

"I didn't know that," said Papa Bear.

Mama Bear asked, "But how does that help us?"

"Yeah," said Bob Bear. "How does that help us?"

Goldy responded, "Rump will work out the details, like how much our company is worth. Then he'll make new shares to sell to people..."

Bob Bear said "New shares? So we Bears will still own the company, plus we get money from these new shares and this Rump guy?"

Goldy said, "That's right, Bab...er, Bob. Rump's company NeverRipOff will make *new* shares of 3 Bears B&B. We'll all agree on a reasonable price for the new shares."

"So...what happens then?" Bob Bear asked.

Goldy said, "Then, Rumpelstiltskin NeverRipOff will add part of my shares, too. After that, he will sell the new shares, and mine, to people who want to invest in the 3B's Just Right B&B Company."

"Oh, my goodness," Mama Bear said. "There are lots of those."

"You get the money you need for your expansion plans and I get money, too," said Goldy.

Mama Bear said, "People keep telling us, 'You Bears have a gold mine here. We'd sure like a piece of the action.'"

"Well, now," Goldy said, "they can buy it!"

On the advice of Rumpelstiltskin, thirty *new* shares would be offered to the public, of which fifteen were Goldy's. The remainder of Goldy's shares would stay with the company because, as Rump told the four,

"It doesn't look good to the people who are buying the shares of the new company if the venture capitalist wants to leave the company altogether. They think, 'What's wrong with 3Bears Just Right B&B if one of the major shareholders wants out?'"

So Rumpelstiltskin NeverRipOff set about figuring out a reasonable price for the new shares and setting the date for the big sale.

It was an *enormous* success. Because this was the first time the public was able to own part of the 3 Bears Just Right B&B, it was called ***an initial public offering or IPO.***

At the celebration party, Rump told the four, "This was my best deal ever! I'm so pleased."

Goldy and the Bears were pleased, too. After all, Goldy still owned a large part of the new company, but she also got the money from the 15 shares she sold on the IPO. The Bears got the money from the 15 new shares of the company. Now they could fix up the inns and add more.

"What's not to like?" they asked each other.

The Bears and Goldy gleefully high-five'd with fist bumps all around. Then Goldy went to her desk and began to pack up her stuff. Despite the offering's success, the Bears looked sad.

"We'll really miss you, Goldy," said Mama Bear.

Papa and Baby added, "Sure will. Sure will."

Goldy said, "Oh, this isn't goodbye, Bears. I'll still see you at our yearly shareholder meetings."

She snapped her little briefcase shut and added, "And now I'll take my farthings and go off to find other adventures."

CHAPTER TWO

BOB BEAR GOES TO WORK FOR RUMPELSTILTSKIN NEVERRIPOFF

When Bob Bear was old enough, he was able to help his mom and dad run the 3 Bears B&B Company, which was now called simply "3BB&B." He liked the hotel business, but he didn't *love* it. One day, he explained this to his parents.

"Mama, Papa, it's been great working with you and seeing the business grow, but now..." he found it hard to go on.

"Yes, son?" both parents asked.

"I, well, I feel the need to *find* myself," Bob said finally.

"'Find yourself?'" Papa said.

"You're...right here, son," Mama said, perplexed.

"I mean, I need to do something on my own. Something other than the hotel business," Bob said.

"Like what, son?" asked his father.

"I've been talking with Rumpelstiltskin and I think I'd like to go work for Rumpelstiltskin NeverRipOff," Bob said.

Papa Bear and Mama Bear were silent for a few minutes, pondering this idea of their son's. Finally, Papa Bear said,

"That's a worthy business, Bob. I think you'd be very good at it, too."

"You'd be very good at *anything*, son," said Mama Bear.

So both Bears gave Bob their blessing, and Bob Bear went to work for Rumpelstiltskin as a *stock broker*. A stockbroker is someone who buys and sells shares of companies for people who want to become *investors* in public companies.

The years went by. Rumpelstiltskin and Bob Bear became close friends, despite their age difference. Rump was like a kindly uncle to the young bear.

"There is a lot to learn, my Bear," Rump had told Bob on his first day at work, and indeed there was. Bob carried his training manuals home every night and studied hard for the exam he had to take in order to work for RNRO.

"You don't just say 'shares' now," Bob Bear said to his parents over the dinner table. "You say 'shares of stock'. Anyone can be an investor as long as he or she has the money to buy 'stock'."

"I'm not sure I understand, son," said Mama Bear. "You are working in Rumpelstiltskin's stock store?"

"Well, sort of..." said Bob Bear. "Except we don't call it a store. It's called the *Stock Exchange*. We exchange our investors' money for shares of stock when they *buy*...and shares of stock for money when they *sell*.

"Yes, yes," said Papa Bear who had been reading Bob's training manuals, too. "The stock *market* represents all the companies that buy and sell their shares for public investors, not just 3 BB&B. The Stock Exchange is the actual place where that happens."

"An interesting business, son," Papa Bear concluded.

After Bob Bear passed the exam to become a stockbroker, Rump set about guiding Bob's new career and giving him good advice.

One day, Rump called Bob Bear into his office. With a proud smile, he told the young Bear,

"You've got the gift, Bob. You're a born salesbear. Like me, you can make anything sound good. You, too, can spin straw into gold."

Rump paused, puffing on his cigar. Then he went on.

"But with that gift comes responsibility, young Bear. *Big* responsibility. That is why I named my firm 'NeverRipOff.' We *never* rip off our clients, *never*. Ours is the most trusted investment firm in the entire industry."

Rump reached into his desk and took out an important-looking document. Handing it to Bob Bear, he said, "Please take this important document and keep it where you can read it every day."

Bob Bear took the paper and read aloud, "Rumpelstiltskin's Rules for Making Your Farthings Grow."

Rump said, "I want you to memorize these Rules and follow them very carefully."

He walked around his desk and put his right arm around Bob Bear's big, furry shoulders. He swept his left arm around the RNRO office and said,

"Someday, my Bear, this will all be yours. I want you to run it as well as I have, keeping in mind always that our firm is called 'Rumpelstiltskin NeverRipOff.'"

"Yes, Uncle Rump, sir. I will do that," said Bob Bear.

Rump returned to his desk, took a seat, and gestured for Bob to do the same. Then he said,

"Tell me, Bob, did you ever hear how Goldilox got her start in investing?"

"No, I didn't. I'd sure like to know that," said Bob.

"You've heard of the legendary Tom the Turtle, of course?" asked Rump.

"Of course," said Bob. "Everybody's heard of him."

"Back in the day, he was a great help to Goldy," Rump said.

"Really?" said Bob. "How?'

"I'll tell you how, because Goldy's story illustrates my very first rule well," said Rump.

Bob referred to the document he held in his paw and read aloud, "Rule #1: Get Started and Keep Going. Slow but steady wins the race."

He looked up from the paper and said, "Tell me about this one, Uncle Rump."

"Happy to, my Bear," said Rump.

CHAPTER THREE

TOM THE TURTLE and RULE # 1
Get Started and Keep Going. Slow but Steady Wins the Race

"So true," said Rump. He leaned back in his chair, took a puff on his big cigar, and began his story.

"When Goldy was a young girl (she was still called by her real name back then which was Ethel), she showed little interest in spending her allowance on trifles like tinder boxes or magic beans."

"'I'm saving my farthings,' she told me when I visited her one day. She was standing at her kitchen counter, on which lay a large pile of gold farthings," Rump said.

"I've got..." she was counting her coins, "... wow! I've got 483! That's a lot of farthings!"

"Indeed it is, dear Ethel," Rump told her.

At that moment, Goldy's rich neighbor, Tom the Turtle, came by for tea. He noticed the gold coins rolling around on the kitchen counter.

"Keep those farthings there, Ethel, my friend, and someone will steal them," Tom the Turtle told her.

"But I'm saving them," Ethel said.

"What are you saving them for?" Tom asked.

"I don't know," said Ethel. "But I'm going to keep on saving my farthings, until I have something I want to spend them on."

Tom said, "Oh, you can do that and more...but not by keeping your fortune in your cupboard. Or on your kitchen counter."

"Right," Ethel said, gathering up the coins. "I'll put them under my mattress."

"No, no, no, that's not a good idea either," said Tom. "Have you considered spending your farthings for shares of stock?"

"Not really," Ethel said. "Seems too risky."

"Keeping them in the cupboard or on the counter or even under your mattress is even riskier, my friend," Tom told her. Fingering one of the gold coins, he went on, "If I'd done that, I never would have become the rich turtle you know today."

Tom paused, then he said, "You remember my experience in the King's Forest Footrace years ago?"

"Sure," said Ethel. "The only other runner in the race was that blowhard bunny named Harry the Hare. Sure, I remember."

"Right," said Tom. "Because Harry the Hare was famously swift, all the other would-be runners were discouraged from entering the King's Forest Footrace."

"He was swift, all right," said Ethel. "I remember seeing him shoot out ahead of you right at the starting line."

Tom said, "Harry was so far ahead of me that he was just a speck in the distance. When he finally paused for breath, that blowhard bunny decided to take himself a little nap."

"That was dumb," said Ethel.

"True," said Tom. "Because while he was sleeping, I finally came plodding along and just kept on going past him, lumbering by in my slow but regular turtle way."

Tom smiled at the memory. "You see, Ethel, my dad always told me, 'Son, we're *turtles* and we're *slow*. But if you just get started and keeping on going in life, you'll find out that slow but steady wins the race every time.'"

"That's good advice for a turtle," said Ethel.

"That's good advice for *anyone*," said Tom.

"I remember that you got to the finish line first," said Ethel.

"Before Harry even woke up," said Tom.

"I remember the announcer was so excited," said Ethel. "He said over his microphone, 'Folks, we have a surprise winner! In a stunning upset, Tom the Turtle will be awarded the cash prize of one thousand farthings...by the King himself!'"

"It was a grand moment," Tom said.

"Your dad was very wise," said Ethel.

"Yes," agreed Tom. "He also told me that the only way a common turtle like me could ever become rich was to invest that money I won wisely. So I applied my Footrace experience to that effort, investing my winnings in solid companies."

"How did you know which ones were 'solid'?" asked Ethel.

"Because they were earning more money every year, slowly and steadily," said Tom. "They remind me of *me*, these companies...'Slow but steady wins the race,'" he said. "I wanted to get rich, sure. But I didn't want to 'get rich *quick*'. My dad told me that's a good way to also 'get *poor* quick' when things don't go well for a flashy business. I wanted to 'get rich slow.'"

"...ly. Get rich slow*LY*," said Ethel.

"Right," said Tom. "Get rich slow*ly*. I knew I had to get started on investing and to keep going, just as I had in the King's Forest Footrace."

"So what did you do next?" asked Ethel.

"I took my winnings to Rumpelstiltskin NeverRipOff, of course," said Tom. "Rump's business is to buy and sell shares of stock for his clients. Which he did for me. And in the fullness of time, I was actually richer than all the turtles and even all the hares in all the land."

"Wow, Tom! I'm going to heed your advice," said Ethel. "I'll miss counting my farthings every day, but I do want to get rich slowly."

"Which she did," said Rump to Bob Bear. "She invested all 483 farthings, plus all the other money she got from her allowance and from babysitting and delivering newspapers, with Rumpelstiltskin NeverRipOff. Rump bought solid companies for her, which made more money every year but made it slowly and steadily."

Rump went on, "Eventually she did so well that people began to call her "Goldilox" because she had so much gold. We became good friends."

Rump put his feet up on his desk and smiled at the memory.

"She said to me, 'I've got so much money now, Rump, that I can find new businesses which haven't gone public. I can become a *venture capitalist* and have lots of adventures helping new businesses offer their stock to the public in an IPO.'"

Bob Bear said, "An initial public offering!"

Rump went on, "Right. 'Rump,' she said, 'I'm going to go out into the world and find great *private* companies in which to invest if they'll have me.'"

Rump tapped the long ash on his cigar into a little dish. "You remember what that means, Bob? When people can't buy shares of a company because it isn't public, it's called a "private" company. Adventure capitalists give money to private companies and help them grow bigger. When a private company needs money and wants to offer part of itself to the public, and when the adventure capitalist wants to move on to other

RUMPELSTILTSKIN'S RULES FOR MAKING YOUR FARTHINGS GROW

private companies, it 'goes public'. Like you and your folks did with 3Bears Just Right B&B."

"I remember," said Bob. "Goldy told us she was an adventurous capitalist. Venture capitalist for short."

"And she was a very good one," replied Rump. "Although still just a young girl, she found many opportunities to help young companies go public. One of her most successful ventures was... well, I guess that's where this story really began...with the 3Bears Just Right Bed & Breakfast Inns."

Rump continued, saying in his this-is-important voice, "So, Goldilox and Tom have both always insisted that I begin my list of rules for successful investing with Tom the Turtle's dad's advice,

'Get started and keep going and remember that slow but steady wins the race.'"

CHAPTER FOUR

THE THREE PIGS and RULE #2
Always Ask What Could Go Wrong

Bob Bear referred to the list he held in his paw. "Tell me about this one, Uncle Rump. **Investment Rule #2: Always ask, 'What can go wrong?'**"

"Will do, my Bear." Rump settled back in his chair. "I think the experience of the Three Pigs will explain it best.

"You see, once upon a time, there were three pigs who lived in extreme poverty with their single mom.

"She was an unemployed pig, without a barnyard or a trough from which to eat. The local farms where Ma Pig once worked had been sold and turned into shopping malls and housing developments."

"I hate it when that happens," said Bob Bear.

Rump went on, "With no barn to live in, Ma and her three piglets had to stay under a bridge, sleeping on an old mattress someone had tossed there. It was an awful place, but at least it was dry

when it rained and under shade when the sun beat
down on the little family.

"Years later, Ma Pig told me her story."

"For food to eat," Ma Pig said, "I was forced
to snuffle through other people's garbage which I
found in cans and piles in the alleyways behind the
shopping malls.

"Every day, my three little pigs sat under
the bridge and waited for me, their Ma, to come
home with something for them to eat."

Ma Pig sighed at the memory. "It was a
terrible way to live. I dreamed of a better life for
me and my three little pigs."

She brightened, continuing with her story.
"One day, while I was trotting through the back
streets of the village, I came upon a building on
which was posted a sign. It read, 'We Pay $$ for
Bottles and Cans! Bring your Recyclables Here!'

"Hiding behind an open door, I watched in
fascination as people arrived with armloads of
bottles and cans. They disappeared inside the
building with their trash and came out counting
money.

"I was thrilled! I trotted quickly back
through the alleys I had come to know so well,
collecting all the bottles and cans I could find.

"Then I entered that building," Ma told Rump. "There, just inside the door, sat a wizened old man. He took my bottles and cans and handed me a fistful of *money*!

"I was filled with joy. I trotted back to my three little pigs and immediately hid that money in the springs of the old mattress."

Rump told Bob Bear, "From that day forth, Ma Pig left the bridge early every morning and returned late every night with money from the wizened old man.

"Finally, one day when all the springs of the old mattress were stuffed with money, Ma Pig called her sons together.

"'Boys,' she said. 'you are no longer piglets. You must take this money and go out to seek your fortunes.'

"'But, Ma...,' whined the Youngest Pig.

"'No 'but, Ma's',' said Ma Pig. 'Your Ma is no longer young. And while I don't mind picking through those garbage cans all day - that's kind of fun for a pig - I am sick and tired of living under this bridge.

"'What we need,' Ma declared, 'is an actual *house* to live in.'

"Her three pigs looked at each other in bewilderment. 'A house?' they asked.

"'Yes, my Pigs. A house,' said Ma.

"At this," Rump said, continuing with his story, "the two youngest pigs immediately began to argue about who would get to choose the house for their Ma.

"The Eldest Pig told them to *shoosh*. He was a more worldly and sophisticated pig than his brothers.

"He said, 'Ma, you're dreaming if you think we can buy a house with that money. Real estate prices have gone through the roof in this village.'"

Ma Pig's face fell. She squatted on a nearby log and looked at the rocks and dirt and squalor of their makeshift home under the bridge.

"Then I don't know what we're going to do," she said to her sons, holding her head in her hands.

"Well, I *do*," said the Eldest Pig. "We're going to invest this money in the stock market. We can buy shares of stock in public companies which are doing well, and our shares will grow in value, too."

"Where is this market?" Ma Pig asked her eldest son. "I know this village pretty well. I know the produce market and the fish market and the meat market, but I've never seen or heard of any stock market."

The Eldest Pig said, "We don't go to the stock market ourselves. It's far far away. We go to a stock...*broker*."

"A what?" asked Ma Pig.

"A **stockbroker**," repeated her son.

"Someone who breaks these share things? Why would we do that?" asked Ma Pig.

"No, no, no. A stockbroker is a person who buys and sells shares in companies, for customers like us. We won't get rich overnight, but it's the only way I know for simple pigs like us to get rich eventually."

Ma Pig was uncertain. She looked at her three sons and asked plaintively, "No chance one of you might find a princess to marry?"

"Be realistic, Ma," said the Eldest. "Look at us. We're *pigs*."

This was indeed true. So, it was agreed that each pig would get his share of the money Ma had earned and would take it to a stockbroker to buy shares in good companies.

The youngest and, frankly, the dumbest pig took his money to an unscrupulous broker who told him,

"You will get rich overnight if you buy stock in this new company, Sturdy Straw Dwelling Places. It builds houses out of ...*straw*! Very cheap to produce. This company is going to make a fortune for its shareholders! Buy *now!* Before its stock takes off and doubles, triples in value!"

The younger pig (and the dumbest) was so excited at the idea of getting rich overnight and making his fortune so easily, that he didn't ask a single question. He handed over all his money and ran home to tell his ma and brothers what he'd done.

The very day after the youngest pig invested all his money in Sturdy Straw, the company met with disaster. The three pigs and their Ma heard a newsboy shouting from the street corner,

"Read all about it! 'Sturdy Straw Shuts Down After Wolf Blows Away Model Home!'"

Ma Pig bought a paper from the boy and read aloud the awful news, "Sturdy Straw management and workers were horrified last evening when a wolf, a disgruntled former employee, arrived at the model straw home mumbling incoherently, according to witnesses.

"Then he shouted, 'I'm going to huff and puff and blow your house down!'"

"To the horror of the onlookers, that's exactly what the wolf did."

The article went on to say that the wolf had been fired for his whistle-blowing report to authorities that the Sturdy Straw houses were unsafe and could be easily destroyed by a stiff wind.

The youngest pig snatched the paper from his Ma and continued reading aloud, "The wolf escaped in the confusion following the house's collapse. Sturdy Straw's stock closed down, losing 90% of its value!"

He was crushed to read this horrible news and dropped the paper in dismay, saying, "I am *penniless*."

Ma Pig was so angry with the youngest pig for not being more careful with the money that she shouted at him, "Go to your mattress this instant!"

The youngest pig slunk off in disgrace.

Coincidentally, the middle pig had also invested in housing. He was intrigued when another unscrupulous stockbroker told him,

"The future is in sticks, bro. Buy stock in Super Stix Homes today! Sticks are plentiful and they make great insulation. This company is going to soar in value. You, as a stockholder, will be rich overnight!"

The middle pig wasn't much smarter than his brother and failed to ask any questions. He bought the stock in Super Stix Homes and ran home to tell the others.

Two days later, the wolf hit Super Stix. Same M.O. Same warning.

"I'm going to huff and puff and blow your house down!" once again, the wolf was heard shouting, with the same result.

The Super Stix model home collapsed, just as the straw house had done, under the gusty force of the wolf's huffing, puffing blow. The wolf once again escaped capture.

That night, the wolf called the host of a popular evening call-in show, claiming credit for the collapse of Super Stix - both the model home and the stock for it lost most of its value after the attack.

He said to the host, "Wolf, here. Say, I really enjoy your show. Thanks for taking my call. Yeah. I'm the one. Yeah. I did it, and I'll do it again.

"See, I'm an activist wolf and I'm going to expose the weakness in these dwelling places before the people get hurt and lose more money." With this, the wolf hung up before his call could be traced.

The Middle Pig, along with the other shareholders, lost nearly all his money in the debacle. He, too, had to bear his mother's anger when she heard the news. He, too, had to go sit on his mattress while his Ma wept in frustration.

Fortunately, the Eldest and smartest pig learned from his brothers' mistakes. He was also interested in investing in housing. So, he went to an honest stockbroker who worked for Rumpelstiltskin NeverRipOff. This honest stockbroker suggested that he buy stock in the fine old firm of Bountiful Brick Hideaways, Inc.

"This company makes homes that withstand wind and weather...and wolves," the honest stockbroker told the Eldest Pig. "The stock in this company should grow over *time*, not *overnight*, but slowly and steadily."

The Eldest Pig was intelligent enough to ask the most important question a potential buyer of stock can ask of a stockbroker, "***What can go wrong?***"

The honest stockbroker thought for a minute and then replied,

"Well, for one thing, as I said, the company won't grow as fast as other flashier companies. So, don't expect to get rich overnight. Business everywhere could slow down and interest rates could go up. These things could keep our company from growing at all. Then the stock would not go up and might actually go down."

The Eldest Pig thought about this. Then he said to himself,

"I like this broker's honesty. Now I know what can go wrong, but I still think that Bountiful Brick Hideaways, Inc. is a good company so I'm going to buy its stock anyway."

The following week it was reported in the newspaper that the activist wolf had apparently attempted to destroy the model home made of Bountiful Brick, even though he had never been employed by or fired by the Bountiful Brick Company. *The wolf had gone rogue.*

The Eldest Pig bought a paper from the corner newsboy and read aloud to his Ma and brothers,

"Around midnight last night, the wolf was once again heard shouting, 'I'll huff and I'll puff and I'll blow your house down!'"By the time the police arrived, he had huffed and puffed so much without success that he himself collapsed and was hauled off to jail."

The next day, Bountiful Brick's stock took off, reaching a record high price by the end of the day and it continued to grow gradually over time.

"Well, Ma," the Eldest Pig said to his Ma one night over the dinner trough, "it didn't happen overnight but I've now made enough money by selling my Bountiful Brick stock to buy the model home of brick for you and my dimwitted brothers."

So the Pig family moved from under the bridge into their new home and lived happily ever after. When unscrupulous stockbrokers, hoping to sell more fly-by-night companies' stock to the two younger Pigs, would beat on the door of their new home, calling, "Let me in, let me in!" all four Pigs, including Ma, would shout back,

"Not by the hairs of our chinny chin chins!"

Rump concluded his story by telling Bob Bear, "As for the three Pigs' investments in common stock shares, they never bought shares in any company without asking questions, beginning with the most important one of all, "***WHAT CAN GO WRONG?***""

CHAPTER FIVE

SLEEPING BEAUTY and RULE #3
Sometimes investors should be loaners, not owners.

Bob Bear said, "That's a cool story, Uncle Rump. I'll always remember from now on to ask what can go wrong with a company before I buy its stock for a client."

Rump said, "Now I have another story for you, my boy...er, bear. As you know, when the three Pigs bought stock, they (along with the other stockholders) became **owners** of those companies. They might have made money (like the Eldest Pig) or lost money (like his brothers) depending on how well or how poorly the companies did."

"Yes, yes," said Bob Bear. "I know that, Uncle Rump."

Rump said, "But suppose clients absolutely couldn't take a chance on losing their money? Suppose they didn't need it to grow but they did need to have it all back at some point in the future?"

Bob Bear paused, thinking about this. "Then I guess they could have loaned the company their money and collected interest on that loan, until the time it is paid back...right?"

Rump was pleased with this reply. "Right you are, Bob! You remember the old story of the Sleeping Beauty, of course."

Bob Bear said, "Sure. Everyone knows that one."

"Well," said Rump, "maybe everyone doesn't know that her tale is a good example of my third investment rule."

"Sometimes investors should be loaners, not owners."

Rump went on to explain, "Here is the way Sleeping Beauty's story really happened."

This is the story Rump told Bob Bear:

When the little Princess, Beauty, was born and about to be baptized, the King and Queen didn't have the forethought to invite the meanest fairy in the kingdom to the baby's fancy christening party.

Well, actually, they did consider it, but immediately decided against sending her an invitation.

"The Mean Fairy is such a sourpuss," said the Queen.

"Yes. She's nasty, too," the King added.

So, they crossed the name of the Meanest Fairy in the Kingdom off the list with a bit of a flourish.

Now, this was really dumb of them because the christening was the biggest social event of the season that year and *naturally* the Mean Fairy heard about the party from the other fairies as soon as they got their invitations.

The Mean Fairy was furious to think she hadn't been invited. For days before the christening, she stomped around her fairy aerie, enraged.

"It's not like *I* don't like to get dressed up, too," she said to her parrot (because she had no friends to complain to). "It's not like *I* don't like to go to fancy parties, too. It's not like *I* don't like to eat fancy food and maybe dance a little like those prissy little good fairies."

The Mean Fairy's face wrinkled into an even deeper frown than usual. She snarled, "I'm going to do something really *mean* to those people."

The day of the party arrived. All around the kingdom courtiers, townspeople, and fairies were fluffing themselves up and climbing into their best outfits for the big event.

The Mean Fairy brooded as she looked out her window at the carriages rolling down the street on their way to the castle. She just *had* to think of something to spoil this party to which she hadn't been invited. She paced back and forth, wrapped in deep, dark thought. What could she do to wreak her revenge? Finally, an idea came to her which was *really* mean.

"I've got it!" she told her parrot. "I'm going to put my worst mean-fairy curse on the *baby*!" She cackled with glee. "I'm going to put the kid in a *coma*. I'll make her sleep like she's *dead* for ten...no, twenty...no, thirty years! Heh heh heh heh!"

The Good Fairy, the kindest and best-loved Fairy in the land, was rushing by the Mean Fairy's window at exactly the moment when the Mean Fairy uttered these words. She was horrified.

"Who would do such a thing to a baby?" she asked herself. "But I know that Mean Fairy well enough to know *she's* the one would do it. That fairy is so mean! I must counteract this awful curse, if I can." The Good Fairy hurried on to the castle.

The Mean Fairy threw on her cloak and
dashed out to be across the moat before it closed.
When she entered the castle itself, she pulled the
cloak over her head, so the King and Queen
wouldn't know that she had crashed their party.
Then she hurried into the large hall, where the
King and Queen were sitting on their thrones with
their Princess Baby on her own little chair at their
feet.

Each party-goer was laying a gift on the
floor near the thrones. Soon, there was a pile of
dolls and toys and board books and frilly little
dresses.

Mean Fairy stepped forward, threw back
her cloak and snarled,

"I have a *special* gift for the baby Princess,"
she said.

The King and Queen looked at each other in
horror.

"How did *she* get in?" they asked.

The Mean Fairy gave her nastiest laugh
causing the Princess Baby to shriek. She spoke
loudly to be heard over the shrieks.

"I'm placing a curse on Princess Baby which
will put her into a coma...a deep sleep, like she's

dead. But not right away." The Mean Fairy turned and pronounced her curse to all the party-goers.

"When she grows up to be a beautiful young woman, she'll prick her finger and fall quickly into a coma, sound sound sound asleep." The Mean Fairy once again gave her nastiest laugh. "Heh heh heh....and she'll stay asleep for *thirty years!*"

"Whaaaaat?" cried the other Fairies.

The King and Queen said, *"Thirty years? THIRTY YEARS?"*

The Mean Fairy gave them a particularly mean smile and pushed her way through the crowd, going off to find the fancy food and drinks.

Now the Good Fairy was determined to outwit the Mean Fairy. The Good Fairy's powers of Good were strong, but not strong enough to undo the curse entirely. She stepped up to the King and Queen who sat stupefied at the Mean Fairy's curse.

"Do not despair," the Good Fairy said. "I will lay on a *counter-curse*. Now maybe the princess will never prick her finger when she is a beautiful young woman. But if she does and the Mean Fairy activates her curse, her fortune, which I understand is absolutely huge, will *disappear*!

"The Mean Fairy will have to give over every farthing to the kingdom for it to use for all the thirty years of her curse on the baby Princess!

The Good Fairy concluded, "Once the Mean Fairy hears about my counter-curse, I am *sure* she will remove hers."

Time passed. Through the years, the Good Fairy made it a point to hang around the castle and to check up on the wakefulness of the Princess. She tried her best to keep pins and needles away from the child, so that she wouldn't prick herself and activate the curse.

But, one day when she had become a beautiful young woman, the Princess plucked a rose from the palace garden and pricked her finger on the stem.

"Ouch," she said. Then *zonk,* the Princess fell to the floor and began to snore. Courtiers tried to wake her, but to no avail. Finally, the palace footmen carried the beautiful young woman to her bed.

The King and Queen hovered over their daughter, wringing their hands and remembering the Mean Fairy's curse.

"Oh, my dear Princess!" said the Queen through her tears.

"Thirty years," said the King in dismay. "She's going to be like this for *thirty years.* That was the Mean Fairy's curse!"

The Good Fairy hustled into the room. "Fear not," she said. "I shall simply activate my counter-curse. Surely the Mean Fairy will undo hers when she realizes she is going to lose the use of her absolutely huge fortune."

Suddenly there was a clap of thunder, a flash of lightning, and a stiff wind which turned into a tiny tornado. Twirling around inside it was the Mean Fairy.

The tiny tornado spun over the moat and through the castle gate and into the palace where it dropped the Mean Fairy at the feet of the King, the Queen, the Good Fairy, and a lot of startled courtiers. She was carrying a large briefcase and look even angrier than usual.

She picked herself up, brushed off her fairy suit and wings, and hurled the large briefcase at the Good Fairy.

"There!" she shouted. "That's *everything.* Every farthing I own. You have left me farthing-less!"

"Undo your curse," the Good Fairy demanded. "Awaken the Princess and you shall have your farthings back."

"I can't do that, you idiot," said the Mean Fairy, "any more than you can undo yours. Don't you know *anything* about curses, you fool of a Fairy?"

The Good Fairy was crestfallen. "Well, no," she said. "I'm *good*. Why would I?"

The Mean Fairy stepped back into the tiny tornado which had been waiting for her in the corner of the throne room.

"*I'll see you in thirty years and I'd better get back every one of those farthings, or I'll curse this whole kingdom into smithereens!*"

With this, the Mean Fairy twirled away, leaving the King, the Queen, and all the courtiers in stunned silence. The Good Fairy rushed to the large briefcase and lifted it up. It was heavy, very heavy. She set it down again and opened it to view its contents. The King, the Queen, and all the courtiers drew near to see. *The briefcase was stuffed with gold farthings.*

The Good Fairy ran her fingers through the top layer of farthings.

"We can't just keep this money lying around the palace in this large briefcase," she said. "There must be a million million million farthings in here. The kingdom can do a lot with this money."

"Oh, my, yes," said the Queen. "The village needs a new bridge and roads and schools. And the palace could use some serious refurbishing."

The whole court looked at the sleeping princess.

Then the King said, "Thirty years isn't so long. We can keep her dusted and change her dress now and then..."

The Good Fairy was silent for a moment, thinking about how they could use all those farthings, but still be certain the Mean Fairy would be paid back in thirty years.

Then she snapped her fingers and said, "I've got it! I know just what to do with this money so the kingdom can use it for the next thirty years."

The King said, "But wait! We have to give every single farthing back in thirty years or we'll be smashed into smithereens."

All shuddered at this thought.

The Queen was wringing her hands in despair. "How can we possibly do that if we spend all the money?"

The Good Fairy reassured her. "Never fear! I'm going to invest it all in a triple-A rated 30-year *bond*," she said. "It'll pay us interest twice a year and we can use that money for the kingdom.

"When the bond comes due in thirty years, we'll get back all of the Mean Fairy's farthings because the bonds will be triple-A rated which means they are very, very safe!"

Good Fairy hefted the briefcase onto her back. "I'll be back!" she cried. "I'm taking this large briefcase to Bruce, our town's stockbroker. As you know, he is an excellent fellow and he works for the local branch of Rumpelstiltskin NeverRipOff. Bruce has handled the investments of all of us fairies and has always given us good advice."

Then the Good Fairy twirled out of the castle and down the street to the office of Rumpelstiltskin NeverRipOff. There she found Bruce sitting behind his desk.

The Good Fairy plopped the large briefcase on the desk and told Bruce about the Good Fairy's initial curse, the Mean Fairy's thirty-year curse, and the Kingdom's need for the million million farthings in the briefcase. She concluded,

"It is extremely important that we have them all back in thirty years, or the Mean Fairy will smash us all to smithereens," she told Bruce. "Even you, Bruce."

But Bruce was not dismayed. He said, "I do believe I can be of service, Madam." Sitting back in his chair, he said in a soothing voice, "You're dealing with dual curses, as I understand it?"

"Yes," said the Good Fairy. "The King and Queen want to fix up the palace and the town with this enormous pile of farthings, but they also need to have the whole pile back, intact, in thirty years."

"Yes," Bruce said thoughtfully. "I see the problem."

"I thought maybe **high-quality AAA-rated thirty-year bonds** would do the trick," said the Good Fairy. "Am I right? Would they work?"

Bruce replied, "You couldn't be righter, Good Fairy. We can make sure that the Mean Fairy gets all her money back in thirty years by buying a triple-A rated *Treasury* bond. As you know, when you buy bonds, you are actually loaning money to the bond issuer who promises to pay back when the bonds "mature." In this case, the bonds would mature (and pay back the loan) in thirty years. For the privilege of having the money you loaned, the issuer pays 'interest' which is a percentage of the bond's value."

Bruce went on, "And the good news is that the kingdom can use that interest payment, which comes twice a year, to do all the things the King and Queen want to do - to fix the bridges and roads and refurbish the palace."

"Yes," said the Good Fairy. "I know all that. But to whom should we lend the Bad Fairy's million million million farthings?"

"Ah!" said Bruce. "I have just the right borrower in mind. We'll buy the 30-year treasury bonds issued by the far-off country of Usa. They always need money."

"Usa?" asked the Good Fairy. "Where is Usa?"

"As I said, it's far-off. But their treasury bonds are of the highest quality. They are backed by the full faith and credit of the Usa government. The Usa government has the taxing power to pay back the bonds by taxing its many citizens. That's why their bonds get the triple-A rating."

"And you can loan money to Usa for AAA bonds for their treasury even though Usa is far-off?" asked the Good Fairy.

"Oh, yes," said Bruce. "These bonds are sold to many kingdoms."

"This is very good news," said the Good Fairy. "But there's one thing I must ask you before turning over this large briefcase of farthings."

"What's that, Good Fairy?" asked Bruce.

"What can go wrong?" she said.

"Ah! The most important question an investor can ask!" Bruce said. "Well, it is unlikely, even impossible, that Usa could not collect enough taxes to pay the interest on its bonds and the Kingdom is not going to sell the bond before it matures."

"Therefore," Bruce continued, "I have to say, and I don't say this lightly, in this particular case, there is nothing that can go wrong," he said.

"Okay," said the Good Fairy. "That'll work. Let's do this thing."

And it did work. Bruce arranged for the Good Fairy to lend (in the name of the Kingdom) all million million million farthings to the far-off government of Usa.

In return, the Good Fairy received an official-looking paper with fancy gold borders on which were written the terms of the loans, the amount of interest to be paid twice a year and the date thirty years hence, when all the farthings would be paid back to the Mean Fairy.

Then she hurried back to the palace where the King and Queen were waiting anxiously.

"I've got the bond!" the Good Fairy told them, and all three hurried to the Kingdom's vault. They carefully lay the AAA-rated, 30-year Treasury bond issued by Usa inside of the vault, where it stayed for the next thirty years.

During those years, while the princess snored peacefully on her little bed, the King and Queen received the interest payments paid to the Kingdom twice a year and refurbished the Palace, fixed up the bridges, roads, and schools and were even able to give the Royal courtiers and town workers much-needed pay raises. Five percent of a million million million farthings is a lot of money!

Finally, at the end of thirty years just when the bond was about to "mature" and pay back the million million million farthing loan, a handsome prince rode into town on a sleek white horse.

He galloped up to the palace to pay his respects to the King and Queen who were in the Great Hall, hovering around the bed where lay a beautiful princess.

Hurrying inside, the Prince called out to the King and Queen, "Ho, there!"

The King and Queen looked up, startled to see him.

"I am Prince..." he began. The he peeked around the pair and saw the sleeping princess. He was so dazzled by her beauty that he rushed past the monarchs and kissed her gently on the forehead.

That was the very moment that the Usa bond "matured," which means came due and paid off. The Mean Fairy arrived, twirling into the palace in her tiny tornado and headed for the Palace counting room where she received every farthing of her huge fortune. She could be heard by all cackling with glee as she counted the farthings.

"...nine gazillion, ninety-nine patillion, ...ten trippety tatillion...million million million. Okay!" she shouted. "It's all here. It's all here! It's all here!" Stuffing her farthings into the enormous bag, she twirled into the Great Hall, doing a little happy dance.

The King and Queen said to her, "Uh, about the curse?"

"Oh...right," the Mean Fairy. She twirled, waved something (maybe a farthing) and said, "The curse is *lifted!*"

The Princess stretched and sat up in her little bed to the delight of her parents and all the courtiers and, of course, the handsome Prince.

(To this day, the Prince is convinced she awoke because of his kiss.)

In due time, the two were married and naturally lived happily ever after. So did the entire kingdom, thanks to the 30 years' use of the Mean Fairy's farthings in the form of a AAA-rated, 30-year Treasury bond.

It had worked perfectly because, as stated in Rumpelstiltskin's Rule #3, **Sometimes people should be loaners instead of owners.**

CHAPTER SIX

THE EMPEROR'S NEW ROBE and RULES #4 & #5

Always understand how a company makes its money. RULE #5: Never never pay too much for its stock. (Beware irrational exuberance; never confuse brains with a bull market)

Rump sat back in his chair and said, "So what do you think, Bob? Do my investment rules make sense to you?"

"I sure can understand now why you'd want to ask, 'what can go wrong?'" said Bob. "And I know to beware of stockbrokers who can't give you straight and honest answers. I'm glad to know about bonds, in cases when it's better for an investor to be a loaner instead of an owner, but..." Bob sat down heavily on his own chair. He sighed, looking bewildered. "But...," he said again, hesitant to go on.

"What is it, my Bear?" asked Rump, gently.

"There's something about this business that I've never been sure of," Bob said. He held his big head in his paws.

"Ask me. Go ahead. I'll do my best to explain if I can," said Rump.

"See, it's like this, Uncle Rump," Bob began. "I really like buying stocks and being an owner of companies, although I know it can sometimes be better to be a loaner. It's exciting to watch your money grow, but..." Bob looked uncomfortable.

Rump said, "But sometimes it doesn't, right?"

Bob said, "Right. Sometimes..." he shuddered, "it *shrinks*."

Rump smiled. "Often that's because you didn't really understand how the company made money, or if it even made money at all," he said. "When that happens, you can find yourself paying *waaaaay* too much for the company's stock.

"As you know, I hate to pay too much for anything, but especially for stock. If people decide they don't want it, like anything else, it goes on sale at the end of the season."

Rump stood and walked around his desk. He put his arm on Bob's big furry shoulder and said in a stern voice, "Therefore, you must *always always* understand how a company makes it money and you should *never never* pay too much for that company's stock."

Rump continued, "I think you know the story of the Emperor?"

Bob asked, "The one with the new clothes?"

"Yes," Rump said, "that's the fellow. But his story is a little different than the way it was reported in the media. And it is a fine example of my next two investment rules. Please pay close attention to these."

Bob consulted the list he held in his hand. He read,

"Rule #4. Always understand how a company makes its money.

Rule #5: Never never pay too much for its stock. (Beware irrational exuberance and *never confuse brains with a bull market*)

Rump returned to his chair behind the desk and told Bob Bear this story:

Once upon a time, there was a land so far-off that it was ruled by an Emperor instead of a King. This Emperor was known throughout his Empire for his brilliance. He set the trends for business and for fashion. His palace was full of the very latest high-tech gadgetry, and he wore the most stylish clothes. The Emperor, it was well known, was highly intelligent.

"This new gadget," he often proclaimed, holding high a new gadget, "is the Widget of Tomorrow!"

Sometimes the Emperor would appear in a brand-new robe. "And this fine new robe is the Fashion of Tomorrow!" he'd crow.

Because of his reputed brilliance, the Emperor was also known to be able to spot the fastest-growing companies and to make many, many millions of dinars (which was the currency of this far-off land) by investing his money in them.

"I am so brilliant," he once announced, "that I bought Widgetry Inc. for two dinars a share, and now it is selling for 43 dinars a share. How about that, little people?"

The courtiers all applauded with enthusiasm. They were very proud of their Emperor. They watched him closely and listened to him carefully and tried to do everything he did so they could be just like him: stylish, modern, and highly intelligent.

One day, two mysterious-looking men appeared in town. They were hauling between them a large suitcase which bumped along the cobblestone street, making such a clatter that it attracted the attention of Horace, the town's most successful merchant.

Horace had always considered *himself* to be a highly intelligent person, because he made it a point to keep up with the Emperor's every new idea. Now he peered out his window, looking down the street at the two mysterious men.

"Hmmmm," he murmured to himself. "I wonder who those two mysterious men are. I'll just follow along to see what they're up to."

Horace hurried out to the street and followed the two men to the Emperor's palace. There he hid behind a nearby lamppost and listened as one man said to one of the two guards at the Palace gate, "Ho there, Guard."

"Ho, yourself," said the Guard. "Who might you be?"

"We have come from the far reaches of the western beaches of the Empire," they said.

Horace was excited when he heard this. The far reaches of the western beaches were rumored to be places of new ideas. In fact, it was there the Emperor often found new companies to invest in.

Horace tiptoed up to hide behind a closer lamppost so he could better hear the mysterious men.

The second man said to the guard, "We wish to have an audience with your Emperor. He is the most stylish, the most modern, the most intelligent person in all the land. Our message is for his ears alone."

One of the two guards hustled the mysterious men with their large suitcase into the palace. Horace emerged from the lamppost and sauntered up to the remaining guard.

Trying to appear casual, Horace said, "Uh, ho there, Guard."

He took a fistful of dinars from his pocket and slipped them into the guard's hand. "I'd be grateful to you if you could find out for me who those two fellows are and what is in their large suitcase."

The guard looked down at the dinars in his hand, counted them quickly and then said, "Certainly, sir."

He disappeared into the palace, leaving Horace to pace back and forth in front of the palace gates until the two guards finally reappeared.

"What is it? What is it?" Horace demanded.

The guards looked around to make sure no one else was lurking behind lampposts and listening. Then the first guard said in a low voice,

"It is very, very exciting, sir! I heard these men say that our Emperor is so brilliant that they brought it straight to him because they knew he would recognize its value and buy the stock of the company that makes it. But this is *confidential*. Highly *confidential*."

"But what?" Horace said. "What is so exciting and so valuable? Tell me so I can buy stock in the company, too."

The second guard said, "The two mysterious visitors are salesmen. They brought with them a new product from a new company. It is an especially stylish, fashion-forward, hot weather, tropical-weight robe material."

Horace was disappointed, "But what is so special about that? Our Emperor is *always* dressed in robes which are especially stylish and fashion-forward."

The first guard said, "Well, as we understand it, it's the tropical-weight, hot weather part of the material that is so special. It's, uh, it's…"

He consulted a piece of paper. "I wrote it down so I wouldn't forget..." He read slowly from the paper. "It's made with 'a technology which only the most highly intelligent people can understand.'"

Stumbling a little over the words, the guard continued, "This material is processed with thin film laser technology using specialized rigidized demi-condoozers to penetrate the chaps at a rate of 2000 magna boots up to 1000 giganta boots, producing clothing so lightweight and airy, you think you're wearing nothing!"

The guard paused, looked up at Horace who was leaning toward the two expectantly.

"Go on! Go on!" Horace said.

The guard went on, "And the truly special thing about this material is that only the most highly intelligent people will be able to detect its lightweight and airy presence on the body."

The guard paused again and said to Horace, "That's why they brought it to our Emperor, of course."

Horace was silent, then he said slowly, trying to sound as if he had understood any of what the guard had told him, "Well, now. That's extremely interesting."

He took the paper from the guard's hands and read, "'Specialized demi-condoozers,' eh? All the rage, I hear. All the rage," Horace nodded sagely. He read on, "'Up to 1000 giganta boots.' That's a *lot* of giganta boots."

The second guard nodded in agreement and reached for the paper. "A lot of," he looked at the paper, "giganta boots! Sure is!"

"What is the name of this company?" Horace asked. "I would like to buy its stock and become an owner of it, too."

Once again, the guard consulted the paper. "It's the Specialized Materialized Rigidized Tech Corporation. They called it SMART, for short."

"SMART," Horace repeated. "That's very smart!"

He slipped a few more dinars into each guard's outstretched palm and hurried away from the palace, down the road to the center of town. There Horace lumbered into the Empire's branch of Rumpelstiltskin Never Ripoff.

Bentley was NeverRipOff's only stockbroker. He lived in town with his wife, Dora, and their small son, Tommy. He was pleased by the appearance in his office of Horace, the town's most successful merchant.

"SMART!" cried Horace to Bentley. "I want to buy SMART!"

"Good thinking!" said Bentley. "Buying smart is the way to investment success." He picked up his order pad and look up expectantly.

Horace said, "Buy me a hundred shares of Specialized Materialized Rigidized Tech Corp! Called SMART for short!"

Bentley said, "I don't know that company, but wouldn't it be smarter to find out first what could go wrong with it?"

"Nonsense!" said Horace.

"Well, if you say so," said Bentley doubtfully. "It's just that you should always consider what could go wrong with a company's stock before buying it."

"You heard me, my man. Buy me a hundred shares of SMART!" Horace demanded.

Bentley sighed and began writing down all the information he needed in order to buy stock in the company called Specialized Rigidized Materialized Tech for Horace while Horace told him about the two mysterious strangers and their visit to the palace.

When he had finished, Bentley said, "I'm curious about this company called SMART for short. I'd like to be able to tell others about it."

When Horace had left, Bentley saw the two mysterious men, hauling their large suitcase down the street in front of his office.

He ran to the door. "Ho there!" he said to the men.

"Yesss?" they hissed.

"I wonder if you could tell me more about the company SMART?" Bentley said, "...and its product? You see, I'm a stockbroker. And I always want to find out what could go wrong with a company before buying its stock for people."

The two mysterious men sniffed contemptuously. "Wrong?" they said. "Why, *nothing* could go wrong with this product."

They spoke rapidly together. "It's made with thin film laser technology using specialized rigidized demi-condoozers to penetrate the chaps at 2000 magna-boots up to 1000 giganta boots producing a material so light and airy, only the most highly intelligent people can see it or feel it on their bodies."

Bentley said in a small voice, "Uh...I don't understand."

The men chorused, "You *don't?*"

"Er, no," he said.

Then one of the men said to him, "You need to smarten up, buddy. You don't want these people or the Emperor to think you're a fool, do you?"

Bentley shuddered. "No, no, of course not," he said.

"Then get on board, boy," said the other man. "The Emperor himself, a brilliant man, has bought a large number of shares in our company."

"Not only that," said the man, "but we are going to the palace workshop to make the emperor an entire wardrobe of this miracle material which, by the way, is only visible to the most intelligent of folks. In just a few weeks, he will wear his new clothes in his annual Parade for the People."

He continued, "You'll see for yourself just how miraculous this material is but *only* if you are intelligent enough. SMART is the Technology of Tomorrow! Be smart and buy its stock today!"

Then both mysterious men continued dragging their large suitcase down the road.

"Oh, my," said Bentley. "I certainly don't want people to think that I, the sole representative in this far-off land of Rumpelstiltskin NeverRipOff, am not highly intelligent. But I still don't know what could go wrong with the company known as SMART for short."

"I don't even know if the company actually makes any money from their exciting new technology. If I don't know how many dinars this company makes every year, how am I to know whether its stock is cheap or expensive?" he asked himself.

But to Bentley's dismay, no one seemed to care whether the company was even making money at all or if its stock was cheap or expensive. Once the townspeople heard that the Emperor AND Horace had bought the SMART stock, they, too, wanted to own it.

They flooded Bentley's office, demanding, "Buy me a hundred! Buy me two hundred!"

"Oh, my!" Bentley said to Mrs. Bentley. "The **supply** of this stock is not as great as is the **demand** for it. Every time I put in an order for more stock, the price climbs higher. All this buying is making the price of the stock go up and up and up.

"And I still don't know if the company is making money or not. This is making me very nervous."

By the time the Parade for the People rolled around, the price of a share of SMART was over 300 dinars, up from just a few dinars when Horace first bought it.

Bentley was worried about this. He hadn't been able to talk anyone out of buying SMART stock and he was pretty sure it wasn't a good idea for people to keep on buying it without knowing any of the answers to "what can go wrong"?

For other stocks, Bentley could figure out if their prices were reasonable or not. He had a secret formula which he had already taught his little son, Tommy.

BENTLEY'S SECRET FORMULA

Now the price of SMART stock was going up every minute of every day. Tommy who hung around Bentley's office sometimes after school asked his dad,

"Why is that stock going up, Daddy?"

"Because there are more buyers than sellers," said Bentley, as he adjusted his glasses.

Tommy thought about this, "I don't understand. *Why* are there more buyers than sellers?" he asked.

"Because the buyers *think* the stock price will go up and they can then sell it for more money than they paid for it," said Bentley.

"But what makes the stock price go up, Daddy?"

"Good question, son. In the case of SMART, the price is going up because people think that just because the Emperor bought it, they should buy it."

"That's not really 'smart' of the townspeople, is it, Dad?" said Tommy.

"Heh heh. Definitely *not* smart, son," said Bentley. "You have to really understand things *or* ask lots of questions until you do. You can't just believe someone if what they say makes no sense to you and they won't explain it."

"Well, what *is* a 'good reason' to buy a stock, Daddy?" asked Tommy.

"If the company is earning more money each year, the stock price will reflect that. More earnings each year, higher price for its stock. Always happens," said Bentley.

"Oh." Tommy was silent for a minute. Then he asked, "How *exactly* can people tell if the company is earning more money each year?"

Bentley said, "After the company pays all its bills for the year, it divides what's left among the shares of its stock.

"This amount is called the 'earnings per share' or EPS. The EPS of a company is also in lots of newspapers and business magazines so people can check to be sure. Do you follow this far, son?"

"I think so," said Tommy. "So, people can tell that the company is earning more money each year if the EPS is going up?"

"Right you are, son. But how *fast* the earnings are growing is just as important."

"How can people find out how fast the earnings are growing?" Tommy asked.

"Well, if they look at what the company earned last year and what it's expected to earn this and next year..."

"Wait, wait, wait!" said Tommy, because he wanted to understand everything. "Just how do they know that?"

"That's another good question, son, but you really don't have to worry about figuring that out yourself. There are people called '**financial analysts**' who work that out," said Bentley.

"Anyway," he continued, "if people see the difference between last year, this year, and next year...if, say, the fine old company of Bountiful Brick earned $1 last year and is expected to earn $1.10 this year and $1.21 next year, that means the EPS are growing at a 10% rate. Do you see that, son?"

"I do," Tommy said. "The difference between each year's EPS is 10%."

"I'm proud of you, son," Bentley said.

"But why is that important?" asked Tommy.

Bentley leaned in, looked around, and said in a low voice, "Because there is a little formula, a kind of secret way to see if the stock's price now is too high or too low or just right, like the porridge Goldilox found at the three Bears' house."

"Listen carefully, son," Bentley cautioned, "here is my secret formula: *If the stock price when divided by the current EPS is the same or close to the same as the rate at which the EPS are growing, the price of the stock is just right.*"

"The stock price divided by the current EPS is called the P (for 'price') E (for 'earnings') or 'PE'," Bentley said.

Tommy asked, "So if the PE is the same or close to the same as the rate those E's are growing, the stock price is just right, right?"

"Right! Very good, son, very good!" said Bentley proudly. "Now if I tell you that Bountiful Brick is selling at $10 a share, can you use the secret formula to tell me if that's a high, low, or just right price?"

"Sure can, Dad!" said Tommy proudly. "Bountiful Brick is going to earn $1 this year so that's a..." he looked at his dad, hesitating for just a minute, then said, "...PE of 10."

"Yes?" said Bentley. "Go on."

"and the earnings are growing at 10%, like we said," Tommy said.

"Yes, yes," said Bentley. "Continue."

"Well, Dad, that's easy! The PE is equal to the growth rate in earnings! So the price of Bountiful Brick at $10 a share is just right!"

"You got it, son. You got it and I'm so proud of you! Sometimes it's hard to remember that you're only seven years old!" Bentley crowed. "You will make a wonderful stockbroker. Rumpelstiltskin would be very proud of you, too," he added.

BACK TO THE STORY

On the morning of the Parade, Horace woke early. He was excited to get to his place in the reviewing stand. This was the day when the Emperor would be wearing his new robe made of the light and airy SMART material, the robe that only the most intelligent people would be able to see.

Horace was confident that the sight of the Emperor's new clothes would inspire more people to buy the SMART stock.

"Then the price will go up even more and I'll be even richer than I am now," he said to himself.

The clock struck noon. Crowds gathered along the Parade route. Horace and Mrs. Horace hurried to the reviewing stand. "We can stand here, my dear," Horace said to his wife, pointing to a place on the first row of the stand. This was where the Emperor usually stopped and waved to all of his people, allowing them to see whatever fashion-forward style of tomorrow he had chosen to wear that year.

Horace said, "I can't wait to see *this* year's fashion, made of SMART material!! Which, of course, I will be able to do because I am highly intelligent."

Everyone in the crowd was also certain that he and she, too, would be able to see the SMART robe the Emperor was wearing.

There was a brief hush when the band began to play. The strutting horses appeared, ridden by the guards in fancy red and gold uniforms. Then came the footmen bearing colorful banners, finally the band itself, tubas and trumpets and lots of snare drums, blowing and tooting and beating away their marching songs.

The excitement of the crowd was at a fever pitch when finally, walking slowly, sedately, and of course, regally, the Emperor appeared in all his glory...*and nothing else.*

At first the crowd was silent. Then Horace spoke up, loudly so all could hear. "What a magnificent robe our Emperor is wearing! See the way the light and airy material drapes so, er, lightly and airily!"

The townspeople cried, "Of course! We see it! So light! So airy! It's...gorgeous!"

At that moment, Bentley arrived with his small son Tommy. He edged his way through the crowd. Hoisting Tommy onto his shoulders, he asked,

"Can you see, son? Can you see the Emperor? Can you see his new SMART robe?"

Tommy shouted down to his father, pounding on Bentley's head, "Daddy! Daddy! Look! The Emperor! He's *naked*!"

Bentley, who couldn't see anything, called up to his son, "Hush, son. Only the most intelligent people can actually *see* his clothes."

"But he doesn't have any clothes on at all!" insisted Tommy.

The people around Bentley and those in the reviewing stand heard Tommy say this. Then, one by one, they began to murmur. "Dear me. The little boy is right." The murmuring grew louder.

"How peculiar! How puzzling! Wait a minute! How horrifying! We've been FOOLED!"

Now the Emperor realized the truth of what Tommy said, too. He turned around with as much dignity as he could muster, then he rushed down the Parade route and back to the palace, feeling the air wash over his unclothed body.

The crowd stood in horrified silence. No one felt highly intelligent any more. Then they began to shout, "Our SMART stock! We must sell our SMART stock, or we'll be ruined."

They rushed down the street to Bentley's office. Bentley, having anticipated this as soon as

Tommy made his pronouncement, was already there. "One at a time! One at a time, folks!"

Of course, as Bentley was selling all the SMART stock, the price was going down.

Bentley said to the horrified townspeople, "The *demand* for this stock has disappeared, but that means there is now a huge *supply* of the stock. That is because all of you townspeople and Horace, the leading merchant, and of course, the Emperor himself are trying to sell their shares."

Sadly, Bentley said, "The price of SMART shares is now mere demi-dinars, almost worthless."

Mrs. Horace who stood in the doorway of Bentley's office and who had never wanted him to buy the SMART stock, asked her husband,

"Did you even think to ask what could go wrong?"

Horace tried to remember what the mysterious men had told him.

"Well, they explained about the thin film something or other with magnas and gigantas. It was the technology of tomorrow, for heaven's sake! The Emperor himself bought shares!"

"And did you understand even one word of what those men were saying?" Mrs. Horace asked.

Then Horace said the most intelligent thing he had said in a long time.

"No," he admitted. "I didn't understand anything. But I will next time."

Bentley didn't want to make Horace and the townspeople feel even worse than they already did.

"Hear me, please, people," he said. "It's always wise to know not only *what can go wrong* but also if a company is making money at all and if the price is reasonable."

The crowd was shamefaced and also *broke*.

This is the end of the actual story of the Emperor and his new clothes. The townspeople and Horace and Mrs. Horace returned to their homes. The Emperor in his palace put on some real clothes and, as in most fairy tales, everyone tried to live sort of happily ever after.

CHAPTER SEVEN

RUMPELSTILTSKIN AND GLADYS and
RULE #6
Don't expect more from your investment portfolio than is reasonable: Manage your expectations!

When Rump finished telling Bob Bear the actual story of the Emperor and his new robe, Bob said to him, "Wow. Who knew? I'd heard about the Emperor's new clothes but not about the company that made them or actually didn't make them."

"Yes," replied Rump, "it is a well-known tale, one often heard who buy stock without knowing anything about how the company makes money, or if in fact it does make money. Actually, without understanding the company at all."

"And paying too much for that stock, too. Wow," Bob Bear said again. "Tell me again how you figure out if a stock is too expensive? I got kind of lost there."

Rump said, "You divide the stock's price by its estimated earnings per share. That's called the price-earnings ratio or 'p/e' and it should be no higher than the estimate growth **rate** in earnings per share - how fast the company's earnings are expected to grow in future years according to financial analysts who know the company's business well."

"But everyone bought SMART without it having any E for its P. No earnings to compare to its price," Bob Bear said. "So, they couldn't have figured out if the stock was too expensive at all!"

Rump said, "My point exactly. I often wonder, how could anyone do such a thing? That's why I made Investment Rules #4 and #5."

Both sit in silence for a moment. Then Bob Bear took the list from his pocket and said, "You've got one more rule on this list, Uncle Rump."

Rump glances at the list in Bob's paw. "So I do, my Bear," Rump said. "All the rules are important but this final rule I consider to be the most important rule of all. It's sort of a rule for happiness in life, too."

Bob Bear read aloud, **"Have reasonable expectations for your investments and don't expect them to do more than they are capable of doing."**

Rump said, "In other words, **Don't expect your investments to spin straw into gold."**

"But didn't you...," Bob Bear began, "I mean, I've heard so much about your..."

"I know, I know," said Rump. "The old 'straw into gold' thing. I'll tell you what really happened."

Bob Bear settled back in his chair and waiting for Rump to go on.

"Back when I was a young man growing up in a village not far from here," Rump began, "there lived a poor miller, whose name was Homer. Here is his and, more important for me anyway, his daughter's story."

Now a miller's job is to mill wheat into flour, but try as he might, Homer just couldn't get the hang of it. The barn was a mess with wheat chaff flying all around. The little bit of wheat that the miller managed to actually grind just ended up in messy heaps on the wooden floor. He was really a very *poor* miller.

Homer's beautiful daughter Gladys was also a mess. When she would try to help her father mill the wheat, she would often be covered with wheat chaff herself and would have to pick it out of her mouth and hair.

Gladys was known in our village as the Poor Miller's Daughter, to set her apart from the other daughters in the village whose fathers are *good* millers. Few of the townspeople even knew that her name was Gladys and few cared.

"Except me," said Rump. "I'd known Gladys since she was a young girl, tripping over wheat and chaff and often covered head to toe with the powdery residue. I was entranced by her even if she was always in need of a good dusting. She was, to me anyway, beautiful.

Rump went on. "I, of course, am no studmuffin, nor was I then. Girls didn't find my two-foot tall physique, my long bumpy nose, or my beady little eyes all that compelling. So Gladys, while always polite, never knew of my love for her."

One day, the King came riding through the village on a fine white charger. He called out to the villagers, "Greetings, Village People. I am on a quest for a bride!" He said, "Show me what you got!"

The village folks trotted out their daughters, saying things like "My daughter is an excellent cook" and "My daughter is an expert seamstress." "My daughter loves children."

Homer, staggering out from the local tavern where he spent a good bit of time, overheard the other millers bragging about their daughters. He just couldn't help himself. He hollered to the king.

"Cooking? Sewing? Piffle!" Then Homer swaggered right up to the King's fine white charger and bellowed, "My girl Gladys can..."

Here Homer had to think what it was that Gladys could *do*. She wasn't much of a cook, knew nothing about sewing, and Homer had no idea if she loved children or found them to be tedious brats.

But after just a brief pause, Homer announced, "My daughter Gladys can *spin straw into gold!*"

The village folks brayed with derisive laughter. The King did not. He was interested.

"Hmmm," the King said. Then, "Footmen, hold this man!"

Two footmen stepped forward and grabbed Homer by his arms.

"Bring this man's daughter to the castle's stable at once!" the King said. Then he leaned down from his fine white charger and said to Homer, "I'll give you a chance to prove that you are telling the truth and not lying to your King." Looking menacingly at Homer, he went on. "This would be a *terrible* thing to do. 'Gladys' did you say? That's her name, Gladys?"

Homer nodded vigorously.

The King continued, "Gladys can have the next twenty-four hours to spin the straw in my stable into gold. But you should know that the punishment for lying to your King is *harsh...harsh, indeed.* If by tomorrow at this time the straw is still straw, it'll be the dungeon for both you *and* your daughter!"

King trotted off on his fine white charger. The footmen dragged Homer to his little cottage. They waited outside while Homer entered and found Gladys picking straw from her hair and trying to sweep up the chaff which floated everywhere.

Then in a shaky voice, Horace explained what had just happened. Gladys listened and then cried,

"You said WHAT?"

Homer hung his head in shame.

Gladys said, "And now the King expects me to do this or we'll both be thrown into the dungeon?"

Homer nodded.

"Daaaaad!" cried Gladys. Before she could go on, the footmen knocked on the cottage door.

"Come along, Missy," they said. "The King and his stable full of hay await you!"

"Now I had been hanging around the poor miller's cottage," said Rump, "trying to get the nerve to knock on the door and ask Gladys to come out for a stroll in the woods or to have a cup of herbal tea with me.

"When the footmen came into view with the poor miller, I froze in place. Luckily, the footmen passed me right by, thinking I was just another lawn ornament. I heard the exchange between father and daughter and watched while the footmen led my Gladys away, her father standing uselessly in the doorway, waving goodbye.

"I followed them to the King's stable and once again, froze in place among the flamingos and kitty-cats and other lawn decorations. There I saw one of the footmen lift a large silver ball which sat on a pedestal at the barn's door. He withdrew a key and opened the stable door.

"Then the footman patted Gladys on the shoulder and gently pushed her inside. He relocked the door, replaced the key, and hurried away.

"Once the footmen had gone, I dropped my pose, retrieved the key and entered the stable. 'Ho there, Gladys!' I did a little jig. 'It is I...' Then I paused. I wanted to see if she remembered my name. We had been introduced so many times!

"Gladys looked at me unhappily, picking straw from her ears and hair. She started to sob, hiccupping once or twice. Then she stopped.

"'Are you from the King,' she said to me. 'You look familiar. Don't I know you, uh... Mr...uh..?' she continued when I didn't reply. 'I must tell you, I really don't know *what* my father was thinking. You can't imagine what he expects from me...or what the King expects. I have absolutely no idea how to spin straw into gold. *None. Not a clue.*'"

"Ha!" Rump said. "At last I would get the lovely Gladys's attention. I told her, But I do! And, strange as it sounds, this was true.

"As Goldilox said early in this story, everyone has at least one thing he or she can do well and, as luck would have it, my peculiar talent was that I could spin straw into gold.

"You may wonder how I discovered this," Rump continued. "I mean, who sits down at a spinning wheel and feeds it straw to begin with? It happened when I was just a kid, messing around with my mother's stuff and...I don't know...the idea just came to me, like the time I tried to build a fort with her good china.

"Anyway, I stuffed a fistful of straw onto the wheel, stepped on the foot pedal, and lo! It turned itself into gold! I was dumbfounded. None of my other experiments had ever worked so well.

"My mother was so happy, she didn't even get mad at me for playing with her spinning wheel. She asked me to do it over and over. In fact, every time our farthings ran low, I'd whip out another batch. We kept it a secret, of course. We never told anyone about this odd talent of mine.

"Mother would take a stash of straw, now gold, to the next village and sell it there, so no one knew of the source of our funds in this village.

"But now with poor Gladys, my secret beloved, sitting red-faced on a bale of straw in front of me, ridges of tears running down her flour-dusted face, straw in her ears and hair, I could no longer keep silent.

"'Move aside, please,' I said to her. I lifted a bale of straw and hauled it to the spinning wheel standing in the corner of the room. Here I began to work my magic, feeding the wheel the stiff straw and lifting off the soft golden strands it became. Then I said to Gladys, 'That should do it!'

"Gladys stared at the pile of gold and said in wonder, 'How can I repay you?'

"I was hoping I could tell her of my deep love for her, but the words didn't come. Instead, I heard myself say something really stupid.

"'You can give me the ring on your finger,' I told her. What a dolt! Anyway, Gladys gave me her ring and off I went, leaving her with the gold, the leftover straw, and the prospect of the King proposing marriage to her instead of throwing her and Homer into a dungeon.

"I thought that was the end of that. But I wanted to see what would happen when the King saw the gold, so I once again took my lawn ornament pose and waited outside the barn.

"When the King arrived and saw the gold, he said, 'Well done, my girl! Well done! So well done that I want you to do it again...spin more straw into gold and do it in the next 24 hours. We'll see if this is some sort of trick or if you can *really* spin straw into gold.' and off he went.

"When I opened the door and my lovely Gladys saw me, I waited a brief moment to see if she remembered my name this time, but no.

"'Oh, it's...you!' she said. 'I need you again, Mr. Uh...uh...uh' she stuttered.

"I was so disappointed. To Gladys, it was obvious that I was no more than a straw-into-gold spinning troll, a talented garden ornament. But of course, I did my thing, spinning into the night, joyful just to be near my beloved even if she was pacing anxiously back and forth, muttering under her breath.

"Finally, between batches, I asked Gladys what she was muttering.

"'I was just bemoaning the fact that my father has always had such high and unrealistic expectations of me. I simply want to be a good daughter and do my best but he always wants more...oh, I shouldn't trouble you with my problems, dear Mr. Uh...uh..'

"We heard the sound of the King's carriage. 'They're coming!' I said and hurried out to my spot in the garden, taking my place by the pink flamingos. The memory of what happened next thrills me to this day.

"When the King and footmen stepped into the stable, dragging Homer between them, I went to the window and stepped up on a set of ceramic ducks to peer inside. I heard the King say as he lifted the new pile of spun gold,

'Lovely girl! You did just as your father said you could!'

'She did?' said Homer.

'Now you will be my Queen and the whole Kingdom will honor you, as I will!' said the King.

"But Gladys stood up straight and wiping the excess gold off her dress, said to him, 'Thank you, Your Highness. I appreciate the offer.' Her voice grew stronger as she went on. 'But I ask you, *what fool would marry a man who would have thrown me and my father into a dungeon if I didn't meet your expectations?*'

"Homer and the footmen shuddered at Gladys's forthrightness. Homer said, 'Gladys, what are you saying? This is the King you are talking to!'

"Gladys replied, 'I know, Father, I know. But I have made up my mind. This isn't the work of my hands anyway. It is the work of my dearest...' Gladys searched hard for my name.

"The King, the footmen, and Homer all said, 'It is? Who's work is it? Who might that be?'

"Still Gladys looked blank, then she caught sight of me peering in the window. 'Ah!' she cried,

pointing at me. 'It is the work of my dearest...
Rumpelstiltskin!'

"Later, Gladys told me that my name came
to her in a flash of memory as if she saw it printed
in the air. The King, his courtiers and her father all
turned to look at me.

"'Well, what do you know about that!' the
King said to me. 'I never expected my proposal to
be refused but if this girl didn't do all this (he
gestured at the piles of gold) I guess I'll have to
look for someone else to be Queen. And you, sir,
you can report to work at my palace. I can use your
talents.'

"The King signaled to his footmen and
strode off, leaving me hanging in the window. I
climbed down into the barn and gave my dearest
Gladys a major hug. Then I trotted after the King,
ready to report to the palace for straw-spinning
duty.

"Well, Bob, to finish this story, I must tell
you that my strange ability to spin straw into gold
disappeared as mysteriously as it had come. Try as
I might, the straw remained straw. I broke several
spinning wheels trying to repeat my feat to no
avail.

"When the King saw this, he was upset at first. But then he said to me, 'I'm a fair man and I can see that you tried your best. So, I encourage you to turn your attention from spinning straw to learning about the stock market. It can reap huge benefits which are more reliable than straw-spinning.'

"This became my obsession and I discovered that it was a much more interesting and rewarding pursuit. You know the rest of the story. With the King's help, I established the highly successful firm of Rumpelstiltskin NeverRipOff which has become a model for stock brokerage firms through the land.

"Shortly after the stable incident, Gladys consented to be my wife. Our marriage has been a fine one. Indeed, we actually have lived happily ever after."

"This is due to something I learned early in my career, Bob," Rump said. "I offer it as my last rule. It is the secret of a happy marriage and also a successful stock portfolio. One should have *low expectations* for both of these."

"Really, Uncle Rump?" asked Bob Bear.

"Well, I should rather say, *reasonable expectations*. For everything in life, but *especially* for your investments. In other words, you shouldn't expect your company's stock to sell at a price much higher than its 'PEG ratio.'"

"As well as following all your rules for making your farthings grow, right, Uncle Rump" Bob Bear said.

"Now, Bob, my Bear," said Rump as he took the list from Bob and returned it to his desk. "Can you remember all of them without looking at the list?"

"Sure can, Uncle Rump," and Bob Bear proceeded to recite all of them.

1. Slow but steady wins the race.

2. Always ask, what can go wrong with an investment?

3. Know the difference between a loaner to and an owner of a company.

4. Always understand how a company makes its money.

5. Never pay too much for shares of a company's stock.

6. Don't expect your investments to spin straw into gold. That is, don't expect more from your investment portfolio than is reasonable.

ADDENDUM: RULE #7

When Bob had finished reciting all the rules, he took the list up again and saw that Rump had added another.

"What's this one, Uncle Rump? **Diversify: Invest for all "seasons".**

"Do you have a story for it, too?"

"No, Bob," Rump said. "I don't have a story to illustrate that one, but it is extremely important," and he proceeded to explain.

"I look at our investment portfolios as I would seasons of the year. By this I mean, for **Summer**, the season when things in our garden out back are growing nicely, I'd invest in growth stocks.

"For **Autumn** when the weather is uncertain (I try never to use the word "fall" when discussing common stock), I buy those types of stocks which have potential for growth but also pay sizable dividends (e.g. Convertible bonds, preferred stocks, REITs) - just in case the stock market does FALL. Stocks which pay sizable dividends are usually the last thing sold in a down market.

"For **Winter**, the season when nothing in our garden is growing and the stock market is stagnant or dismal, I'll own high quality bonds whose income is "fixed", and we'll get our income regardless of the sinking stock market.

"Now for **Spring** - my favorite season of the year because little shoots are coming up in the garden - cold nights, warm days both conducive for growth of those shoots - this is also my favorite piece of our investment portfolios. I want us to own Growth stocks whose earnings are growing year to year when the economy is robust and also conducive for growth.

"So, that's the end of my Rules. Follow them, dear fellow, and you will have happy clients and be a happy investor yourself."

Then Rumpelstiltskin leaned back in his chair, put his feet on his desk and went to sleep.

THE END

STUDY GUIDE

CHAPTER ONE

"*Going public*" is the term used for the process of selling shares, that were formerly privately held to new investors, for the first time. This is also called the "*initial public offering*" or "*IPO*," for short.

When a company is going public, it is the first time shares of the company are offered to the general public. This requires an investment banking firm, like Rumpelstiltskin NeverRipOff (RNRO) to do the legal work, which is extensive. Here are the steps an investment firm takes when taking a company public:

1. The company's board of directors needs to approve the proposal by the company's management leadership. (In the case of 3Bears B&B, the Bear family and Goldy are both management and board directors).

2. Then an investment firm like RNRO is chosen to do all the work involved in going public.

3. All the financial records for the past five years are reviewed by RNRO. Then a

prospectus, which is a booklet with all the relevant information about the company, is reviewed. This includes, among other details, a description of the business and its management, the names of the current shareholders (the Bears and Goldy, in this case), and how the money raised is going to be used.

4. At this point, the investment bank (RNRO, in this case) examines carefully every aspect of the company's business, including its financial condition, its business plan, its labor force and customers. This step is called doing the *due diligence*. The prospectus may need to be rewritten to include results of this examination.

5. Then the rewritten *preliminary prospectus* is given to the Securities Exchange Commission (SEC) and all other stock market regulators (e.g. state securities commissioners). Sometimes the SEC requires additional information before the prospectus is finalized.

6. When all the information has been compiled into the prospectus, except for the offering price, the company and the

investment banking firm will go on a *road show* to talk to prospective investors about the planned IPO. Only a preliminary range of price is on this prospectus, which is called the *red herring* because this proviso is in red print on the front of the preliminary prospectus.

7. The day before the sale begins, the company and the investment firm agree on an appropriate price for each new share. The price is decided by taking into account the price of competitive offerings, the general market and industry conditions, how much money the company requires from the offering. and the excitement surrounding this IPO. Then a *final prospectus* is printed for all the people who buy the shares. Now, at last, the company has *gone public* and its shares will be available for people to buy and sell.

8. The company is now bought or sold (traded) on the *stock exchanges* or on the *over the counter market (OTC)* which is generally, but not always, used for smaller companies.

CHAPTER TWO

Rule #1 SLOW BUT STEADY WINS THE RACE - Get started and keep going!

"Slow but steady", when applied to a company's earnings, implies that the company will deliver earnings growth annually, (in my opinion) a reasonable number to expect is 5-8%. This growth *rate* also implies that a faster growing earnings pattern is harder to maintain and therefore, somewhat risky.

For example, some technology companies excited a lot of interest for a while with earnings growing at a rapid rate because they were coming from very low or no earnings at all, going from small company to mid-sized.

The 3 Bears B&B, starting with just, say, 2 hotels, can grow to 4 hotels, then 8 hotels for a 100% growth rate. Phenomenal!! It's natural that its growth rate of hotels (and their earnings) will slow in the future - 100 % growth is impossible to maintain safely.

How to find the information on a company's earnings growth rate? This history and current information, as well as future estimated earnings per share, can be found in Value Line, available at most public libraries. Also, the past 3 years and current earnings are found at **NASDAQ.COM** by entering the symbol of the company's stock. That symbol can also be found on the **NASDAQ.COM** site. Remember, it is the *rate of growth, not the absolute number, you are researching.*

CHAPTER THREE

Rule # 2 ALWAYS ASK WHAT CAN GO WRONG?

For example, what specific issues could affect the earnings of a company negatively: new regulation, loss of patent, new competition, management shakeup?

What industry issues could affect the earnings of a company negatively: interest rate hikes, international upheaval, weather disasters, government scrutiny, new technology?

(Note: Industry issues can be overcome if the company has predictable and growing earnings. This might be a buying opportunity.)

Another question to ask, but what will probably be told first by the stockbroker: What Can Go Right? In other words, what must happen for the stock to increase in value?

Knowing the answers to these questions helps an investor manage their expectations.

CHAPTER FOUR

Rule #3 SOMETIMES IT'S BETTER TO BE A LOANER THAN AN OWNER

There are many other forms of bonds with lesser-quality ratings than AAA: AA, A, BBB+, BBB, BB, etc. Only BBB+ and higher are considered "investment worthy." The remaining ratings are given to so-called riskier "junk" bonds, the interest and principal payments of which may not be paid due to potential financial problems for the issuer.

Some other forms of bonds are:

- Municipal bonds, which are issued by municipalities usually to pay for infrastructure projects - the interest paid is lower than other bonds because, when issued by the state in which the buyer lives, it is free of federal tax for that buyer.

- Revenue bonds, the interest of which will be paid by revenue from the issuer (e.g. hospitals, toll bridges and highways). Revenue bonds generally carry a single A rating and therefore a higher interest rate, because of the increased risk that the revenue might not be as projected.

- Corporate bonds, which are issued by corporations to fund operations. Very few of these receive a AAA rating and, as with all the bonds, the length to maturity also helps determine the interest rate (e.g. the longer one has to hold the bond before maturity, the higher the interest paid should be).

CHAPTER FIVE

Rule #4 Always understand how a company makes its money.

Sometimes a company's best-known product isn't the one that's profitable for that company. E.g. Some years ago, a restaurant chain was teeming with customers at all times but stock analysts reported that the company was losing money, not making it, as a visitor to its stores might have assumed.

Large corporations which have introduced fancy new technology products may only make profits on older, mature products and may still be losing money on the new ones. Value Line is a good source of information on a company's profitability if any.

Rule #5. Beware irrational exuberance and never confuse brains with a bull market.

Never pay too much for shares of a company's stock.

A useful "formula" is the so-called "PEG ratio" which simply states that the company's price divided by its estimated earnings per share (stated as "P/E "- the "/" being a signal to "divide") compared to its estimated growth rate in earnings per share should be equal to or less.

This is VERY important for the prudent investor to know in order to decide if a price is reasonable for a company's stock. The P/E should be equal to or less than the annual growth rate in earnings of the company.

For example, if a company's estimated earnings for the following year are $1 and the price is $10, the P ($10) divided by the E ($1) is 10. To pay a reasonable price, the growth rate in those earnings should be 10%. That is, $1 next year, $1.10 the following year, $1.21 the year after that. This information can also be found in Value Line.

Sometimes a company is so solid financially that it sells at a "premium" P/E, meaning higher than its growth rate. These companies should be judged on an individual basis, considering always "what could go wrong?"

CHAPTER SIX

Rule #6 Don't expect more from your investment portfolio than is reasonable. Manage your expectations.

For example, if you bought utility or REIT stocks for income, don't expect them to grow in price (although that often happens). If you bought a company's stock because you expected their earnings to grow and therefore, their stock prices to go up, don't expect to get much income from them (although some fine companies pay good dividends, too). Remember the main reasons you bought each stock.

Rumpelstiltskin's 7 Rules for Making Your Farthings Grow.

1. **Slow but steady wins the race.**

2. **Always ask, what can go wrong with an investment?**

3. **Sometimes it's better to be a loaner to than an owner of a company.**

4. **Always understand how a company makes its money.**

5. **Never pay too much for shares of a company's stock.**

6. **Don't expect more from your investment portfolio than is reasonable. Manage your expectations!**

7. **Diversify**

ABOUT THE AUTHOR

For fifteen years (1980-1995), Susan Laubach worked in the investment business as a stockbroker, a branch office manager, and broker trainer. In 2006, after completing her Ph.D. at University of Virginia, Susan returned to her original career in theatre. She has written and performed for Off-Off Broadway, television, and film and is a member of AEA, SAG-AFTRA, and the Dramatists Guild of America.

Susan's book *The Whole Kitt & Caboodle: a Painless Journey to Investment Enlightenment* (Bancroft Press:1996) was recommended by Economics America and called "The most well-rounded source of basic stock information and education" by Better Investing Magazine.

Prior to her career as a stockbroker, Susan taught creative dramatics to elementary and middle school students at Kent Place, Summit, NJ and at Roland Park Country School in Baltimore, MD and was playwright-in-residence at CTA Theatre for Children (AEA) in Baltimore in the late 70's.

In addition, during her years in the investment business and after, Susan has taught many levels of investment education to both adults and young people at The Greenbrier Resort in White Sulphur Springs, WVA (for CSX shareholders) and at Chautauqua Institution, Chautauqua, NY (ages 18 and up), among other venues.

Made in the USA
Middletown, DE
18 November 2019

78656802R00073